Reading/Writing Companion

Mc
Graw
Hill

mheducation.com/prek-12

Copyright © 2023 McGraw Hill

Send all inquiries to:
McGraw Hill
1325 Avenue of the Americas
New York, NY 10019

ISBN: 978-1-26-573386-5
MHID: 1-26-573386-4

Printed in the United States of America.

5 6 7 8 9 LMN 26 25 24 23 22

A

Welcome to WONDERS!

We are so excited about how much you will learn and grow this year! We're here to help you set goals for your learning.

You will build on what you already know and learn new things every day.

You will read a lot of fun stories and interesting texts on different topics.

You will write about the texts you read. You will also write texts of your own. You will do research as well.

You will explore new ideas by reading different texts.

Each week, we will set goals on the My Goals page. Here is an example:

I can read and understand texts.

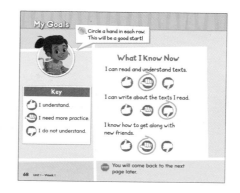

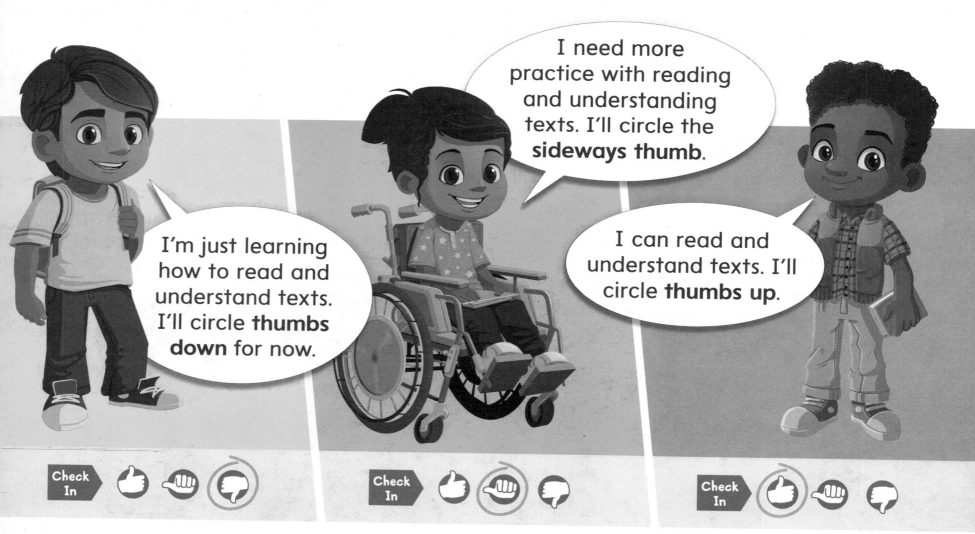

As you read and write, you will learn skills and strategies to help you reach your goals.

You will think about your learning and sometimes circle a hand to show your progress.

Check In

Here are some questions you can ask yourself.

- Did I understand the task?
- Was it easy?
- Was it hard?
- What made it hard?

It is okay if I need more practice. The most important thing is to do my best and keep learning!

If you need more help, you can choose what to do.

- Talk to a friend or teacher.
- Use an Anchor Chart.
- Choose a center activity.

At the end of each week, you will complete a fun task to show what you have learned.

Then you will return to your My Goals page and think about your learning.

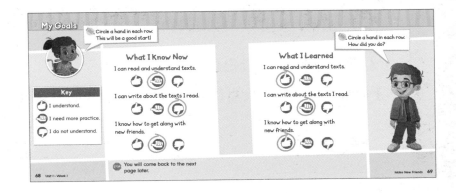

Unit 6 Weather for All Seasons

The Big Idea

Week 1 • The Four Seasons

Week 2 • What's the Weather?

Week 3 • Stormy Weather

Literature Big Book *Waiting Out the Storm*

Paired Selection "Be Safe in Bad Weather"

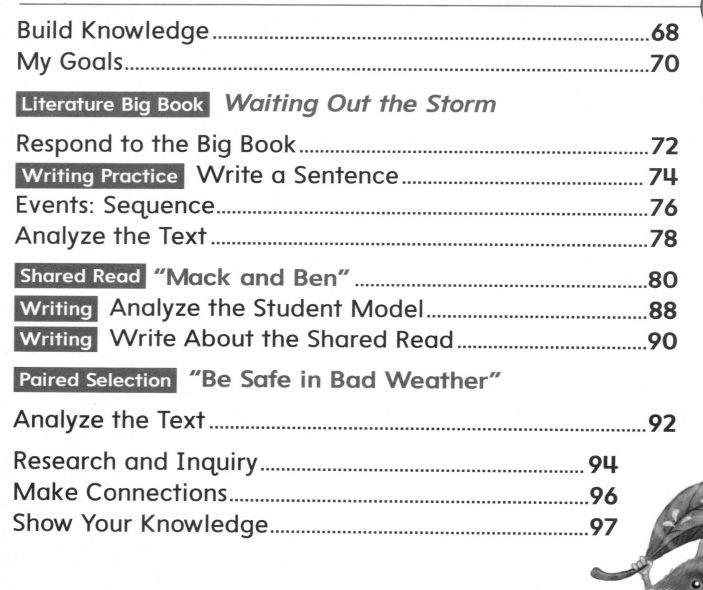

Extended Writing

Connect and Reflect

Creative Crop/Photodisc/Getty Images

Weather for All Seasons

Talk about what the boy and his mother might be saying.

Circle clues in the art that tell what the weather is like.

The Big Idea

How do weather and seasons affect us?

Build Knowledge

Essential Question How are the seasons different?

Build Vocabulary

 Talk about how the seasons are different. What words tell about how the seasons are different?

 Draw a picture of one of the words.

 Write the word.

My Goals

Circle a hand in each row.
It will be fun to learn more.

What I Know Now

I can read and understand texts.

I can write about the texts I read.

I know how the seasons are different.

Key

 I understand.

 I need more practice.

 I do not understand.

 You will come back to the next page later.

Circle a hand in each row.
What are you getting better at?

What I Learned

I can read and understand texts.

I can write about the texts I read.

I know how the seasons are different.

Retell the realistic fiction story.

 Write about the story.

This story is mostly about

_____

- -

_____

Text Evidence

Page

This is realistic fiction because

_____

- -

_____

_____

- -

_____

 Text Evidence

Page

Talk about how you can tell that summer is coming.

 Draw and **write** about one way you can tell that summer is coming.

Summer is coming when

It is not a bit hot!

Hop a lot if it is not hot!

Anya

Write About the Shared Read

Does the author do a good job of showing what winter is like? Why or why not?

 Look at what Anya drew.

 Listen to what she wrote.

Grammar

- A **singular noun** names one person, place, or thing.
- A **plural noun** names more than one.

Ken Cavanagh/McGraw-Hill Education

I think the author does a good job.

I see a funny snowman!

I see the kids hop in the snow.

I like the way the author shows winter.

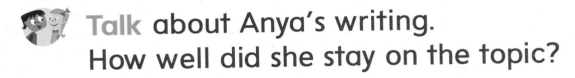

Talk about Anya's writing.
How well did she stay on the topic?

Underline a singular noun
in the second sentence.

Circle a plural noun.

Draw an arrow below the first
sentence from the first word
to the last word.

Writing Trait

When you write,
stay on one topic.

Write About the Shared Read

Does the author do a good job of showing what spring is like? Why or why not?

 Talk about the question.

 Draw your ideas.

Write about your ideas.
Use your drawing to help you.

_____

- -

_____

- -

_____

_____

- -

_____

- -

Remember:

☐ Stay on the topic.

☐ Add singular and plural nouns.

☐ Write from left to right.

Check In 👍 👊 👎

Listen to the poem. Look at the picture. What season is the poet writing about?

 Talk about what a "flying pool" is. How do you know?

 Circle the flying pool.

Quick Tip

You can use these sentence starters:

The poet is writing about _____.

A flying pool is _____.

Talk about the words in the poem. Which words tell what the poet likes about summer?

 Write and **draw** the words.

Words	Pictures

Talk About It

What does the poet not like about summer? Which words tell you? Use the words to make a picture in your mind.

The Seasons

Step 1 Talk about the different seasons.
Choose one to learn about.

Step 2 Write a question about this season.

_____

- -

_____

_____

- -

_____

Step 3 Look at books or use the Internet.
Look up words you do not know.
You can use a picture dictionary.

Step 4 **Draw** and **write** about what you learned.

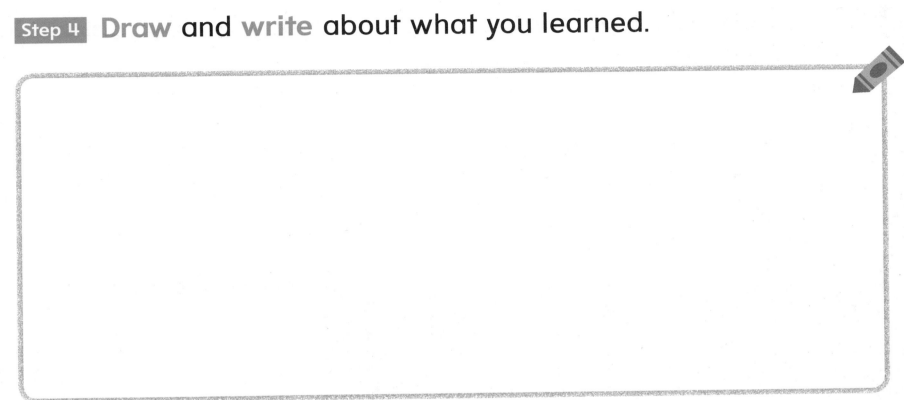

I learned

_____

- -

_____

Step 5 **Choose** a good way to present your work.

Make Connections

 Talk about the painting. What clues help you tell what season it is?

 Compare the season in the painting with the seasons in *Mama, Is It Summer Yet?*

image courtesy National Gallery of Art

Write a Poem

① **Think** about the texts you read. What did you learn about how the seasons are different?

② **Choose** a season. **Draw** a picture of the season.

③ **Write** a poem about the season. Use descriptive words that you learned this week.

Think about what you learned this week. Turn to page 11.

Build Knowledge

Build Vocabulary

 Talk about what happens in different kinds of weather. What words tell about what happens in different kinds of weather?

 Draw a picture of one of the words.

 Write the word.

My Goals

Circle a hand in each row. Whatever you know is okay!

Key

 I understand.

 I need more practice.

 I do not understand.

What I Know Now

I can read and understand texts.

I can write about the texts I read.

I know what happens in different kinds of weather.

 You will come back to the next page later.

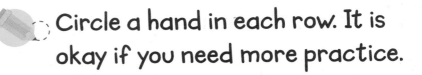 Circle a hand in each row. It is okay if you need more practice.

What I Learned

I can read and understand texts.

I can write about the texts I read.

I know what happens in different kinds of weather.

Retell the fantasy story.

 Write about the fantasy.

This fantasy is about

_____

- -

_____

Text Evidence

Page

This is a fantasy because

_____

- -

_____

_____

- -

_____

 Text Evidence

Page

Talk about how you can tell when the weather will change.

 Draw and **write** about one way to tell.

The weather will change when

What's the Weather? **43**

Writing Practice

Write a Sentence

 Talk about what the animals do when the rain stops.

 Listen to this sentence about when the rain stops.

I splash in puddles after it rains.

 Color the spaces between the words in the sentence.

Writing Skill

Remember:
The words in a sentence have spaces between them.

Write a sentence about what you do
when the rain stops.

_____

- -

_____

- -

_____

- -

_____

Color the spaces between the words
in your sentence.

An author tells the important events
that happen in a story in a certain order,
or sequence.

 Listen to parts of the story.

 Talk about what happens at the
beginning, middle, and *end.*

 Draw what happens.

Beginning

Middle

End

Look at the colors the illustrator uses on pages 12–13.

 Talk about why the illustrator uses these colors. Think about how they help you understand the weather.

Write your ideas.

_____

- -

_____

_____

- -

_____

_____

- -

_____

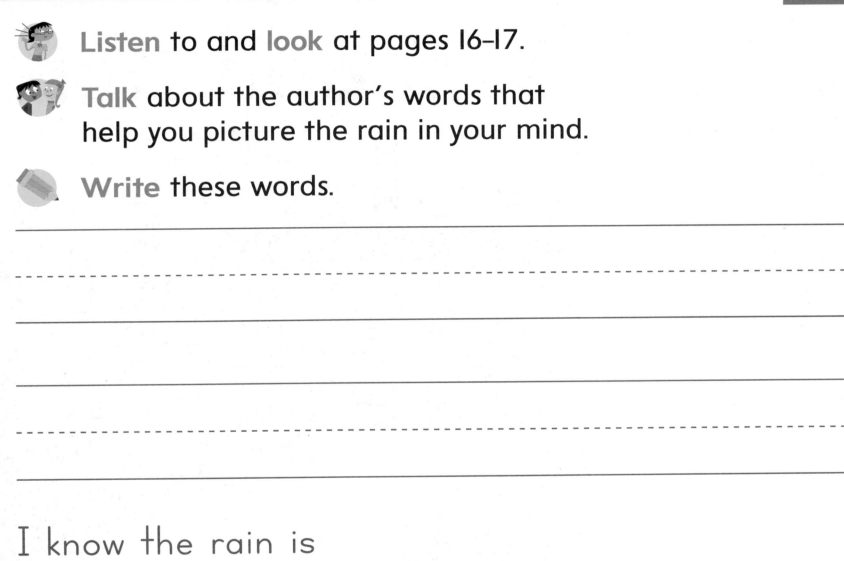

Listen to and **look** at pages 16–17.

Talk about the author's words that help you picture the rain in your mind.

Write these words.

I know the rain is

Find Text Evidence

 Read to find out about Kim and Nan.

 Underline and read the words **She** and **was**.

Kim and Nan

Kim had a lot to pack.

She was a kid on the go.

Shared Read

🔍 **Find Text Evidence**

Read and point to the spaces between the words in each sentence.

Circle who sat on a little rock.

Nan sat on a big rock.

Kim sat on a little rock.

Kim was hot, hot, hot.

Kim had to sip a bit.

Find Text Evidence

 **Circle** the red sack.

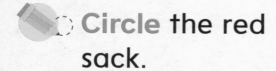 **Talk** about how Nan and Kim feel on page 55. What clues help you know?

Kim had a red sack.

Kim fed a lot.

Nan and Kim sat and sat.

It was not a bit hot!

Shared Read

 Find Text Evidence

 Think about what Kim is thinking on page 57. Make a picture in your mind.

 **Retell** the story. Tell what happens in order.

Kim ran back.

Nan ran back.

Kim has a red pack.

Kim is a kid on the go!

James

Write About the Shared Read

Kim and Nan

What might Kim and Nan do if it is rainy? Write the next part of their story.

 Look at what James drew.

 Listen to what he wrote.

Grammar

A **proper noun** tells the name of a person. *Kim* is a proper noun.

Kim and Nan go to the museum.

First, they see really big dinosaurs.

Next, they learn about stars and planets.

Last, Kim and Nan go to see mummies!

 Talk about how James organized his story.

 **Circle** the words that tell the order.

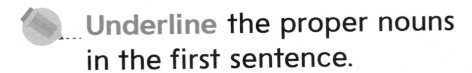 **Underline** the proper nouns in the first sentence.

Writing Trait

The words *first, next,* and *last* tell the order of events in a fiction story.

 Color the spaces between the words in the last sentence.

Write About the Shared Read

Kim and Nan

What might Kim and Nan do on another day? Write a story about their day.

 Talk about the question.

 Draw your ideas.

Write about your ideas.
Use your drawing to help you.

_____

- - - - - - - - - - - - - - - - - - - -

_____

_____

- - - - - - - - - - - - - - - - - - - -

_____

_____

- - - - - - - - - - - - - - - - - - - -

_____

_____

- - - - - - - - - - - - - - - - - - - -

_____

Remember:

☐ Write the events in order.

☐ Use proper nouns correctly.

☐ Leave spaces between words.

Check In

Look at the pictures and words. How does the author tell about the weather?

TUESDAY

It's cloudy, but there is no rain.

WEDNESDAY

Those dark clouds bring rain and storms.

Talk about the weather in each picture.

Circle the picture that shows a storm.

Quick Tip

You can use these sentence starters:

The clouds look _____.

The sky looks _____.

Look at the label on each picture.

 Talk about what information the labels tell.

 Write about this information.

On Tuesday,

_____

- -

_____

On Wednesday,

_____

- -

_____

Talk About It

Why do you think the title of this text is "Cloud Watch"? How do the speech bubbles, labels, and pictures tell about the weather?

Kinds of Weather

Step 1 **Talk** about different kinds of weather. Choose one kind to learn about.

Step 2 **Write** a question about this kind of weather.

_____

- -

_____

_____

- -

_____

Step 3 **Look** at books or use the Internet. Look up words you do not know. You can use a picture dictionary.

Step 4 Draw and write about what you learned.

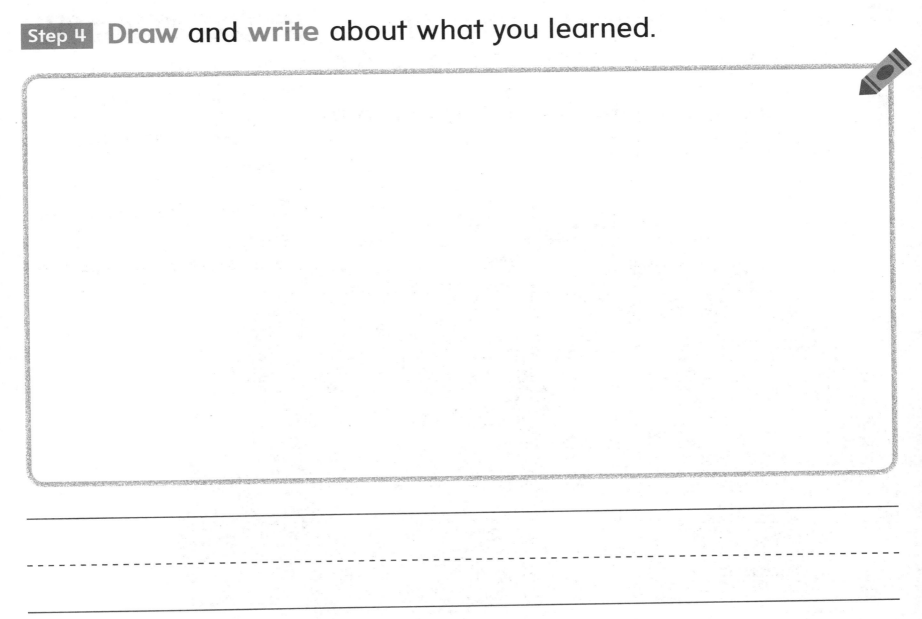

_____

- -

_____

Step 5 Choose a good way to present your work.

Talk about the photo. What clues help you tell what the weather is like?

 Compare the weather in this photo to the weather in *Rain*.

Write a Weather Forecast

1 **Think** about the texts you read. What did you learn about what happens in different kinds of weather?

2 **Draw** what you hope the weather will be like tomorrow.

3 **Write** about your picture. Use words that you learned this week.

Think about what you learned this week. Turn to page 41.

Build Knowledge

? Essential Question How can you stay safe in bad weather?

Build Vocabulary

 Talk about how you can stay safe in bad weather. What words tell about how you can stay safe in bad weather?

 Draw a picture of one of the words.

 Write the word.

My Goals

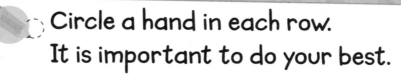

Circle a hand in each row.
It is important to do your best.

What I Know Now

I can read and understand texts.

I can write about the texts I read.

I know how to stay safe in bad weather.

Key

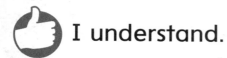 I understand.

 I need more practice.

 I do not understand.

 You will come back to the next page later.

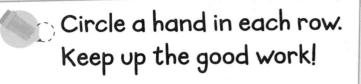 Circle a hand in each row. Keep up the good work!

What I Learned

I can read and understand texts.

I can write about the texts I read.

I know how to stay safe in bad weather.

Retell the realistic fiction story.

 Write about the story.

This story is mostly about

 Text Evidence

Page

This is realistic fiction because

Text Evidence

Page

Talk about stormy weather you have seen. How did it make you feel?

 Draw and **write** about what this stormy weather was like.

Write a Sentence

 Talk about the stormy weather in the story.

 Listen to this sentence about stormy weather.

I see lightning outside my window.

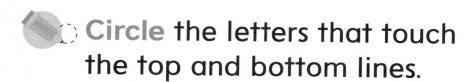 **Circle** the letters that touch the top and bottom lines.

Writing Skill

Try to stay on the lines when you write.

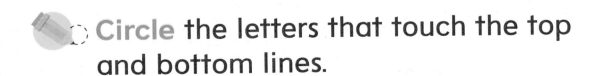

Write a sentence about what you do in stormy weather.

_____

- -

_____

- -

_____

- -

_____

Circle the letters that touch the top and bottom lines.

An author tells the important events in a story in sequence.

 Listen to parts of the story.

 Talk about what happens at the *beginning, middle,* and *end.*

 Draw what happens.

Beginning

Middle

End

Listen to pages 5-7. **Look** at how the words are shown on these pages.

 Talk about why the author uses different kinds of type.

 Write about how this helps you better understand the story.

The different kinds of type help me

_____

- -

_____

_____

- -

_____

Listen to and **look** at pages 26–27.

 Talk about how the girl feels about the storm now. What clues does the author give in the words and picture?

 Draw how the girl feels now.

Find Text Evidence

Read to find out about Mack and Ben.

Circle a word that begins with the same sounds as **sled**.

Mack and Ben

Pit, pat, pit, pat, pit, pat!

Mack ran with Ben.

He did not slip.

Shared Read

🔍 **Find Text Evidence**

Think about what Mack might be thinking. Make a picture in your mind.

Underline words that begin with the same sound as **he**.

Mack was a bit sad.

Ben hid in a little bed.

Mom fed Mack and Ben.

She had a hot, hot ham.

Shared Read

Find Text Evidence

Circle an object whose name begins with the same sounds as **clip**.

Underline words that end with the same sound as **rock**.

The clock can tick, tock!

Mack and Ben sat and sat.

Mack did not hit.

He did not kick.

Find Text Evidence

Circle and read the word **are**.

Retell the story. Use the words and pictures to help you.

Ben can pack a bag.

Mack can pack a tan bat.

Mack can clap.

Mack and Ben are back!

Paula

Write About the Shared Read

What can Mack and Ben do when the rain stops? Write the next part of the story.

 Look at what Paula drew.

 Listen to what she wrote.

Grammar

Remember:
- **Singular nouns** name one person, place, or thing.
- **Plural nouns** name more than one.

The dark clouds go away.

Mack and Ben take their tan bat and ball outside.

Ben throws the ball.

Mack hits the ball with the bat.

 Talk about the descriptive words Paula used in her writing.

 **Circle** the descriptive words.

Underline the plural noun.

 Look at how Paula stayed on the lines when she wrote.

Writing Trait

Descriptive words make your writing more interesting.

Write About the Shared Read

What might Mack and Ben do if it starts to snow? Write a story.

 Talk about the question.

 Draw your ideas.

Write about your ideas.
Use your drawing to help you.

Remember:

☐ Add descriptive words.

☐ Use singular and plural nouns.

☐ Stay on the lines when you write.

Check In

Look at the photos. What clues tell you that a storm is coming?

Whoosh! In some places strong winds blow in spring, summer, and fall, too.

Boom! How can you keep safe if you see lightning or hear thunder?

 Circle the picture that shows windy weather.

 Draw a box around the lightning.

✏️ **Write** about these words.

Whoosh! is the sound of

_____

- -

_____

Boom! is the sound of

_____

- -

_____

Quick Tip

You can use these sentence starters:

Clues in the photo are _____.

I can stay safe by _____.

Talk About It

Look at the Safety Kit checklist on page 32. Why does the author show this checklist? Talk about other things you can put in a safety kit.

Stormy Weather

Step 1 Talk about ways to stay safe in bad weather. Choose one kind of bad weather to learn about.

Step 2 Write a question about how to stay safe in this kind of weather.

_____

- -

_____

_____

- -

_____

Step 3 Look at books or use the Internet. Look up words you do not know. You can use a picture dictionary.

Step 4 Write a list of safety tips you learned.

_____

- -

_____

- -

_____

_____

- -

_____

_____

- -

Step 5 Choose a good way to present your work.

Talk about how this family stays safe and warm. What might the weather be like outside?

 Compare this photo with the ending of *Waiting Out the Storm*.

Goodshoot/Getty Images

Make a Weather Safety Book

1 **Think** about the texts you read. What did you learn about how to stay safe in bad weather?

2 **Choose** one kind of bad weather. **Draw** a picture of that weather. Show how to stay safe in that kind of weather.

3 **Write** about your picture. Use words that you learned this week.

Think about what you learned this week. Turn to page 71.

Writing and Grammar

Pedro

I wrote a realistic fiction story. Realistic fiction has characters who act like real people.

Camping Inside

Min is sad because it is raining.

She cannot go camping.

Min cannot sleep outside in a tent.

Realistic Fiction
My story has a main character and events that could be real.

Then, Min has a great idea.

Min puts old blankets over a table.

"I can go camping inside!"

 Talk about what makes Pedro's story realistic fiction.

 Ask any questions you have about realistic fiction.

 Underline one event that could really happen.

Plan

 Talk about ideas and characters for a realistic fiction story.

 Draw your story idea.

Quick Tip

Think about characters and events that could be real.

Write the name of one character.

_____

- -

_____

Write about an event.

_____

- -

_____

_____

- -

_____

- -

_____

Writing and Grammar

Draft

Read Pedro's draft of his realistic fiction story.

Student Model

A Rainy Day

Min is sad because it is raining.

Min cannot go camping.

Min cannot sleep outside in a tent

Writing Skill

I stayed on the lines when I wrote.

Time Order
I put the events in order.

Then, Min has an idea.

Min puts old blankets over a table.

"I can go camping inside!"

I used a descriptive word.

Your Turn

Begin to write your realistic fiction story in your writer's notebook. Use your ideas from pages 100–101.

Writing and Grammar

Revise and Edit

Think about how Pedro revised and edited his writing.

I wrote a better title.

Camping Inside

Min is sad because it is raining.

She cannot go camping.

Min cannot sleep outside in a tent.

I changed *Min* to the **pronoun *She*.**

I added an end mark.

Grammar

- A **singular noun** names one thing.
- A **plural noun** names more than one thing.
- A **pronoun** can take the place of a noun.

I added a descriptive word.

Then, Min has a ^great idea.

Min puts old blankets over a table.

"I can go camping inside!"

I made sure to use **plural** and **singular nouns**.

Your Turn

Revise and edit your writing. Be sure to use singular and plural nouns and a pronoun. Use your checklist.

Share and Evaluate

 Practice presenting your work with a partner. Take turns.

 Present your work. Then use this checklist.

Review Your Work	Yes	No
Writing		
I wrote a realistic fiction story.	☐	☐
I used descriptive words. They made my story more interesting.	☐	☐
I stayed on the lines when I wrote.	☐	☐
Speaking and Listening		
I listened carefully.	☐	☐
I answered questions. I used details.	☐	☐

Talk with a partner about your writing.

Write about your work.

What did you do well in your writing?

_____

- -

_____

_____

- -

_____

What do you need to work on?

_____

- -

_____

Seasons on a Farm

 Listen to "A Farm Year."

 Talk about weather changes on a farm from season to season.

 Draw two seasons on a farm. Show what happens from one season to the next.

Write about what happens on a farm from one season to the next.

_____

- -

_____

_____

- -

_____

Quick Tip

You can use these sentence starters:

In winter, _____.

In spring, _____.

In summer, _____.

In fall, _____.

_____

- -

_____

_____

- -

_____

Make a Seasons Poster

 Talk about how the weather affects what you do from season to season.

What to Do

1. Draw a picture of yourself in one season.

Show how the weather affects what

you do.

2. Add details.

3. Label the season.

4. Write about how the weather affects

what you do in that season.

You Need

pencil

crayons

Choose Your Own Book

Minutes I Read

 Write the title of the book.

_____

- - - - - - - - - - - - - - - - - -

_____

 Tell a partner why you want to read it.
Then read the book.

 Write your opinion of the book.

_____

- - - - - - - - - - - - - - - - - -

_____

- - - - - - - - - - - - - - - - - -

_____

Think About Your Learning

Think about what you learned in this unit.

 Share one thing you did well.

 Write one thing you want to get better at.

_____

- -

_____

_____

- -

_____

Share a goal you have with your partner.

My Sound-Spellings

Aa a — apple

Bb b — bat

Cc c ck k — camel

Dd d — dolphin

Ee e — egg

Ff f — fire

Gg g — guitar

Hh h_ — hippo

Ii i — insect

Jj j — jump

Kk c k ck — koala

Ll l — lemon

Mm m — map

Nn n — nest

Oo o — octopus

Pp p — piano

Qq qu_ — queen

Rr r — rose

Ss s — sun

Tt t — turtle

Uu u — umbrella

Vv v — volcano

Ww w_ — window

Xx x — box

Yy y_ — yo-yo

Zz z _s — zipper

Handwriting Models

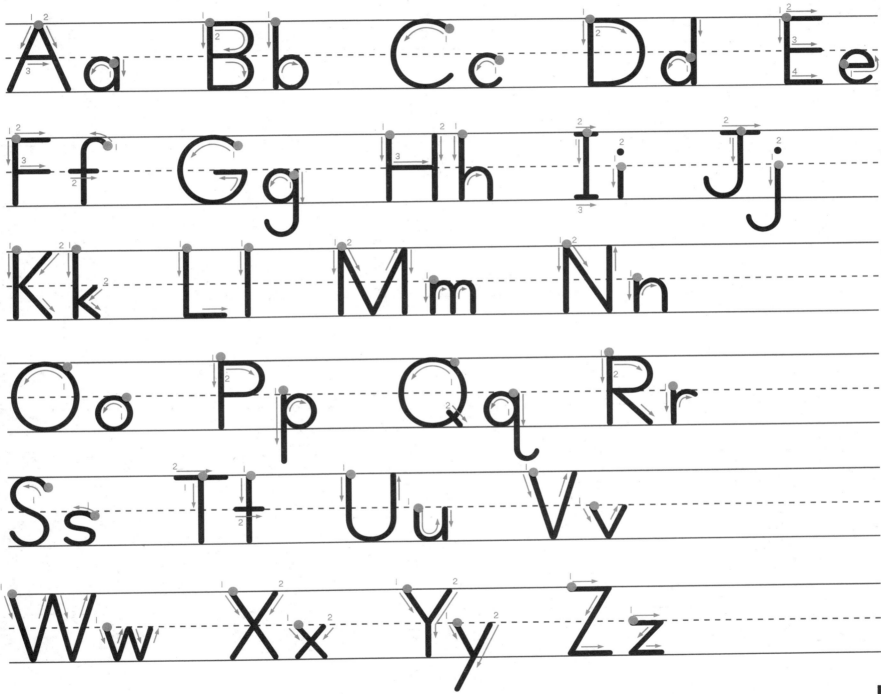